Pebble® Plus

Helping the Environment

I Can Reduce Waste

by Martha E. H. Rustad

raintree

a Capstone company — publishers for children

Raintree is an imprint of Capstone Global Library Limited, a company incorporated in England and Wales having its registered office at 264 Banbury Road, Oxford, OX2 7DY – Registered company number: 6695582

www.raintree.co.uk
myorders@raintree.co.uk

Edited by Anna Butzer
Designed by Kayla Rossow
Picture research by Tracy Cummins
Production by Laura Manthe
Originated by Capstone Global Library Limited
Printed and bound in India

ISBN 978 1 4747 7034 7 (hardback)
ISBN 978 1 4747 7038 5 (paperback)

British Library Cataloguing in Publication Data
A full catalogue record for this book is available from the British Library.

Acknowledgements
iStockphoto: AfricaImages, 15, AzmanL, 11, gradyreese, 21; Shutterstock: Aleksandra Suzi, 5, Aleksei Potov, Cover, Jacob Lund, 13, Kumer Oksana, Back Cover, Lopolo, 17, Monkey Business Images, 7, 9, Ms Moloko, Design Element, Tom Wang, 19

Contents

Keep or throw away?

That rubbish stinks!

Wait, there are useful items
in the rubbish. What a waste!

We can help reduce waste.

Stop wasting food

Our family makes a meal plan and shopping list. We buy only the food we will use. We are careful not to buy too much that will go off quickly.

For meals, we take only what we will eat. After meals, we save our leftovers. I pack leftovers for lunch the next day. We put food scraps in the compost.

Uh-oh! Our bananas have turned brown. We mash them and bake them into muffins. I swirl the bananas into a smoothie too.

Stop wasting resources

We can stop wasting water. I shower just long enough to get clean. I turn the tap off while I brush my teeth.

I can save water outside.
A water butt catches
rain near our house. Later,
Dad and I use the water
in our garden.

I can stop wasting energy.
We turn down the thermostat
by a few degrees. I turn off
lights and electrics when we're
not using them.

To save fuel, I walk or ride my bike to school. We use cloth napkins to save paper. We do not use plastic bags. We take cloth bags to the shops.

Help the environment

We can stop wasting food and water. We can save energy and other resources. Together, we can reduce waste and help the environment!

Glossary

adjust move or change something slightly

compost a mixture of rotting leaves, vegetables and other items that make the soil better for gardening

energy usable power, such as electricity or fuel

environment the natural world of the land, water and air

fuel anything that can be burned to give off energy

resource something useful or valuable to a place or person

thermostat a device that controls the temperature of the air in a building

water butt a large container that collects rainwater from a roof or gutter

Find out more

Rubbish and Recycling (How Does My Home Work?), Chris Oxlade (Raintree, 2013)

Rubbish and Recycling (See Inside), Alex Frith (Usborne, 2010)

What A Waste: Rubbish, Recycling and Protecting our Planet, Jess French (DK Children, 2019)

Website

www.bbc.com/bitesize/articles/z9w26sg

This BBC Bitesize video shows what happens to your litter when it is thrown away.

Comprehension questions

1. Making a shopping list and composting are two ways of stopping food waste. What is another way?

2. Why are plastic bags bad for the environment?

3. How does using cloth napkins stop waste?

Index